ABOUT LADY RED EGO AND XIAOYU LUO

Lady Red Ego (@ladyredego) is a Chinese/Scottish lesbian writer concerned with intimacies. Her first pamphlet, *The Red Ego*, was published in 2019 with Wild Pressed Books and her second pamphlet, *Natural Sugars*, was published in 2020 by Broken Sleep. Her debut collection, *Your Turn to Speak!*, was published in March 2023 with Blue Diode Press.

Xiaoyu Luo was born in 1960 in Xi'an, China. She was the first woman to earn a PHD in fluid mechanics at Xi'an Jiaotong University in 1990. Two years later, she moved to the UK to become a post-doctoral researcher at the University of Leeds, where she later met her husband and fellow applied mathematician, Nicholas Hill. In 2008, she was the first woman to become a professor of applied mathematics at the University of Glasgow. In 2014, she became a Fellow of the Royal Society of Edinburgh.

Xiaoyu Luo lived a full and happy life in Glasgow with her husband, son, daughter, and later, daughter-in-law and grandson. In addition to her scientific career, she was an avid reader of both English and Chinese literature, and towards the end of her life enjoyed blogging and translating texts, including *My Dearest Friend*. After battling lung cancer for six years, she passed peacefully on the 5th of February, 2025.

My Dearest Friend
我最亲爱的伙伴

Lady Red Ego with Xiaoyu Luo

VERVE
POETRY PRESS
BIRMINGHAM

PUBLISHED BY VERVE POETRY PRESS
https://vervepoetrypress.com
mail@vervepoetrypress.com

FIRST PUBLISHED APRIL 2025

Printed and bound in the UK
by Imprint Digital, Exeter

ISBN: 978-1-913917-67-8

For My Mother

母亲致女儿的信：

女儿，你今天毕业啦，获得了一等英国文学学士。22个春秋，弹指一挥间。
记忆犹新，是你的童年。婴儿的你，呀呀学语。两三岁的你，在美国的
一个国际晚宴上丢下目瞪口呆的父母，跳上舞台为上千嘉宾翩翩起舞。掌
声中你高举连衣裙无邪地露出小裤头，吓得我冲上舞台抱你下来。四岁时
我带你参加芭蕾舞班，开车迷了路，停下看地图。你在后面轻轻地说："
妈妈，我觉得你应该多吃点鱼"。哎，谁叫我说吃鱼对脑子好？五岁时你
学会了数码相机，到处照了地上的小石头、墙角、人们的鞋子和后脑勺。

我们一起荡秋千，坐滑梯，读风趣横生的儿童书籍，在每个动人的故事之间
流连忘返。我们把《西游记》一遍遍几乎讲烂，犹不过瘾，就自编自演，成精
作怪。你和哥哥一样，把我再次带回无拘无束的童年。有一天你发现了妈
妈相貌平平，看着我的满脸雀斑纳闷道："为什么爸爸会爱上你呢？"我笑
着说："据外婆说是因为妈妈心灵美"。你想了想，同意了："嗯，妈妈就像
卡西莫多(巴黎圣母院里的敲钟人)。"谢谢你，孩子！我们也一起发
傻，看谁能把脸变得更丑，先发笑者输。你邀爸爸一起玩，他不敢，因为
对手"竞争实力太强！"一次去欧洲旅游，在机场出了安检见到一面明亮
的窗子，我们一时兴起在窗前各种比丑。一会儿突然有人从里面敲窗。原
来窗内的监控人员实在看不下去了！我们尴尬而大笑地跑开。

还记得你八岁那年我们在曼哈顿炎热的公寓里躺在上铺床上一起读《哈利
波特》吗？从那时起你成为忠实的哈粉，并宣布长大要当一名作家。你画
写自己的魔幻小小说，绘声绘色的作品获到了小学校长奖。我对你唯一的
要求是学中文。每年假期带你回国，中国的文化民俗慢慢溶进了你的血液
。现在你讲一口流利国语，能看懂中文版的《哈利波特》，并试尝着用中
文写诗。

十一岁那年我第一次失去耐心吵你。你事后温和地对我说："妈妈，请不
要大声喊我，我不喜欢"。从此我真的没有再吵过你，而你也绝少给我生
气的理由。女儿，你教育了我，令我内疚在你哥哥的叛逆期没做个更好的
妈妈。你慢慢长大，委婉而不失主见。永不说是非，有一群挚友。高中时

我们原想让你学理工, 因为工作好找。但是你选择了文学, 宁可当一辈子穷作家。你认为生活不仅需要谋, 更需要爱。孩子, 知道你要寻找自己, 也知道我们作父母的, 其实无权左右你的人生。你个性鲜明, 讨厌种族、性别、及一切歧视。女儿, 我们无条件接受你的一切, 更殷切希望你和这个尚不平等, 可能 也永远不会完全平等的社会彼此包容。

现在你我早已是无话不说的知心朋友。大三时你去阿姆斯特丹作交换生, 我在金秋的日子里去荷兰看你。母女俩挤在学生宿舍的床上通宵达旦地聊天。我们一起参观梵高博物馆, 去河边的餐馆吃饭, 租了自行车到处玩儿, 最喜欢在林荫葱郁的冯德儿公园里兜风。黄昏后我们散步于宽敞的街道, 在打烊后的商店窗前再次比丑。

女儿, 你也许长大了, 但永远是我心里深爱的小女孩。不企望你成为一个大作家, 但希望你在写作中找到快乐。不祈望你此生毫无波澜, 但希望你的小船驾驭自如。不指望你去赢得世界, 但希望你能征服自己。不望你功成名就, 但愿你为而不争。不奢望你作一颗最亮的星星, 但求你的闪烁长长久久。孩子, 人生漫漫, 此行珍重。请比我更早些明白:爱, 就是珍宝;善, 就是武器;知足, 就是富贵;幸福, 就是成功;健康, 就是王道。

A Mother's letter to her Daughter:

My beloved daughter, today you have achieved a remarkable milestone, graduating with a First Class BA in English Literature. It seems like just yesterday that you were a little girl, and the memories of your childhood are still fresh in my mind. I recall the adorable baby version of you, your babbling and innocence. There was a particular incident when you were two or three years old, where you left your astonished parents at an international conference dinner in the United States and fearlessly jumped onto the stage to dance for the thousands of guests. Amidst the applause, you held up your dress and innocently exposed your pants. I hurriedly rushed up to hug you and bring you down. Another time, when I took you to a ballet class but got lost along the way and you, at the tender age of four, softly suggested, "Mum, I think you should eat more fish." Oh, why did I tell you that fish is good for the brain! At the age of five, you learned how to use a digital camera and filled the memory card with pictures of stones, corners of walls, people's shoes, and even the back of their heads.

We shared joyful moments on the swing and slide, indulged in fun children's books, and immersed ourselves in captivating stories. Your favourite book was *Journey to the West*. We read it countless times, and yet, you never seemed to get enough of it. So, we created and acted out our own sequels, each of us portraying characters like the mischievous monkey, the lovable pig, and the white horse. You added a new character, the little white horse, which became an extension of yourself. Just like your brother, you brought me back to my carefree childhood. One day, you noticed my freckles and wondered, "Why did Dad fall in love with you?" I smiled and replied, "According to grandma, it's because of my inner beauty." After contemplating for a moment, you agreed and said, "Mama is like Quasimodo from the Notre Dame Cathedral." Thank you my darling! We also goofed around together, competing to see who could make the ugliest face

— the first to laugh would lose. When you invited Dad to join in, he declined, jokingly claiming he couldn't because the competition was "just too fierce!" I still recall a time at a European airport when we passed through security before Dad. While waiting for him, we made various ugly faces in front of a shiny window. After a few minutes, a member of security behind the two-way window knocked, unable to bear our antics any longer. We quickly ran away, overcome with embarrassed laughter.

Do you remember when you were eight years old and we read *Harry Potter* together on the top bunk of our hot Manhattan apartment when we visited New York? That was the moment when your love for *Harry Potter* was ignited, and you proclaimed that one day you would become a writer. You began creating your own magical novels, beautifully illustrated with your vivid imagination, and your remarkable works even earned you the Primary School Head Award. My only request was for you to learn Chinese. Year after year, we would return to China, allowing the rich culture and traditions to slowly weave into your very being. Now, you speak Mandarin fluently, read the Chinese translation of *Harry Potter* and even attempt to write poetry in Chinese.

When you turned eleven, I lost my patience and shouted at you for the first time. However, you responded with gentle words, saying, "Please don't shout at me, Mum. I don't like it." Moved by your maturity, I immediately stopped shouting. In fact, you rarely gave me reasons to be angry. My dear daughter, you have educated me and made me feel guilty for not being a better mother during your brother's rebellious phase. You have grown into a tactful yet assertive young woman, harbouring no interest in gossip and surrounded by a close circle of friends. When it came to your A-level studies, Dad and I hoped you would pursue science and engineering to secure better job prospects. We worried that choosing literature might lead to a more challenging path as a writer. However, you firmly believed that life is not just about survival but about love. April, we understand your desire to find yourself, and as parents, we have no right to control your life.

My dear daughter, you have a distinct personality and detest racism, sexism, and all forms of discrimination. We unconditionally accept everything about you and earnestly hope that you and this society, which is still unequal and may never be completely equal, can embrace each other. Today, you and I have become the closest of friends. When you embarked on your third-year exchange program in Amsterdam, I seized the opportunity to visit you during the golden autumn. Huddled together on the bed in your student dormitory, we chatted all night long. We explored the Van Gogh Museum, dined at riverside restaurants, and rented bicycles to explore the city. Our most cherished memory was our bicycle ride through Vondelpark. After dusk, we strolled along the wide and empty streets, once again making our silly faces in front of closed shop windows.

My precious daughter, you may have grown up, but in my heart, you will forever remain my little girl. I don't yearn for you to become a renowned writer, but I sincerely hope that you find happiness in your writing. I understand that life will inevitably bring waves of challenges, but I pray that your boat remains steady. I don't aspire for you to conquer the world; instead, I implore you to conquer yourself. I don't wish for you to achieve great fame and success, but may you find purpose without undue stress. I don't dream of you being the brightest star in the sky, but may your twinkle endure, shining long and high. My dear child, life is a long journey – cherish every step you take. Please understand earlier than I did that love is a treasure, kindness is a weapon, contentment is wealth, happiness is success, and health is king.

With all my love,
Your mother

CONTENTS

My Dearest Friend

我最亲爱的伙伴

My Dearest Friend

And we are back, again,
at the beginning. The way
the body remembers birth,
the delivery, this tumble of limbs
into golden arms and summer,
the inevitable glory of hearing your
voice for the first time, my name
as clear as a bell. Mother. My
dearest friend, after all.

《我最亲爱的伙伴》

我们再一次,
回到起点。
身体记得分娩,
四肢翻滚着
投入金色的怀抱和夏天。
那无法抗拒的荣耀,
是我的名字, 清澈如钟声,
被您第一次呼唤。
母亲, 噢,
我最亲爱的伙伴。

Walnut Tree

And then there was this.

Childhood, a cornucopia
that keeps on giving. Your cheek
pressed to the pillow, orange skin
and freckle, the light from the bedside table
as sacred as a temple candle. I am in the fields
with you, running through the Chinese sun.
Nothing is off limits; you pull the strips right
off the corn kernel, bright as a pearl. In the walnut tree we
hide from boys and eat white walnuts that stain black
on our teeth. You are yang and I am yin, lounging
in the branches of your memory. You give this, too, to me.
I am still just a little girl who looks so much like your
mother with pigtails. Even then I imagine the infinity
of love, which stretches out through history like
a mountain range. In any age I already see
us under the shade, stealing time and giggling.

《核桃树》

然后, 如取之不尽的金矿
是那童年时光。
您的脸颊
压在枕头上。
黄皮肤, 雀斑,
伴着床头的桔光,
如神烛染亮圣殿。
我们在田野徜徉,
穿越中国的阳光, 自由无束。
您剥开玉米棒,
米粒如珍珠般脱落。
我们坐在核桃树上,
躲开男孩们的追逐,
让乳色的汁液,
将白齿染成墨色。
您是阳, 我是阴,
荡漾在您回忆的枝干上。
这回忆, 您全部给了我,
您说我长得像扎马尾辫时的外婆。

即使在那时, 我已想象着
无尽的爱,
如山脉绵延, 将时光伸展。
即使在那时, 我已看到
每一个年龄的我们,
在树荫下,
咯咯发笑, 偷着时间。

Climate Change

It felt like the whole world
should have moved to save you.
Climate change could wait;
the clouds in the sky and
the moon on the waves could stay
as they are. On their course. Let us
find another way. A path where ocean air
breathes health into all your cells.

I looked in your eyes. For the first time
let myself imagine what we could do
with ten more years.

Everything changed. A bird freezes
mid-flight, wings outspread
as my father rings on my screen. Rivers
begin to flow backwards. Frogs leap heel
overhead. Even the wind is still. Something
has changed, an undercurrent below the ground
and the grass trembles. If I press my ear
to soil I will hear every god answer me.

The river is flowing into your veins. You are
a mother after all,
all this is yours. Have you ever heard
the sound of trees praying? How they sway
even as their roots find life deeper
and deeper.

《全球升温》

整个世界都应该来拯救您。
全球升温可等侯;
天空中的云彩, 海浪上的月亮
都可停下。
让我们寻找另一种方法,
让海洋把健康注入您的细胞。
我注视您的眼睛, 第一次
想象未来的岁月里,
我们一起能做的事。
但一切都改变了,
父亲给我打来电话的那一刻,
鸟儿冻结在空中, 翅翼半展,

河水逆流, 青蛙倒跃,
连风都静止了。
是什么改变了,
让暗流汹涌, 小草颤抖?
我把耳朵贴近大地母亲,
听到了每一个神灵的回应。
那河流正注入您的血脉。
毕竟您也是一个母亲,
这一切都属于您。
您听过树木的祈祷吗?
它们摇摆不定,
那些根却
深深地, 更深地,
将生命寻找。

Castro

And yet it doesn't fail me.
On the Spanish borders, the ocean surges
and brings you years in which angels visit;
a grandson, Fang Xian, perhaps I marry –

I remember waking in the morning and
stepping off the hotel steps in sandals,
swallowing sandy yards until I was there,
in the waves, standing where you had stood. A wish
sent off before it had been fully understood
into the sea, carried deep down to where
Poseidon lives. The bad news of a miracle,
swiftly delivered. On my back, floating as
salt stings the cracks in my lips. I am suspended –
the future reforms like a liquid, holding me to the surface.
I am so small

and your love has made you big,
symbolically winged when you are in fact
bodiless. Divine intervention,
you appear, wild and glorious in the sky,
telling me where I am.

《Castro》

它从未辜负过我。
在西班牙边境，大海翻腾澎湃，
带给您那些有天使守护的岁月；
让您看到孙辈，房县，或者我会嫁人 —

我记得清晨醒来，
踏着酒店的台阶，穿着凉鞋，
一步步吞下沙滩，
站在您曾经踏过的地方。一个心愿
在被完全领悟之前就被寄出，
深深沉入波塞冬的居所。
那个奇迹的坏消息，
火速地传递。我仰面漂浮，
海盐刺痛着我嘴唇的裂痕。我悬浮着—
未来像液体一样变幻，
牢牢将我束在水面。
我是如此渺小

而您的爱使您伟大，
象征性地展翅飞翔，
尽管您实际上是
无形的。神迹令您在天空中出现，
狂野而辉煌，
告诉我，我的所在。

Water's Edge

If this wasn't real
the beach would have more sand,
less pebbles. Water drives a hard
bargain, this slow, enervating
disintegration. Fractions stack,
Jenga spines crack. I know that
you are teetering on your last stance.
There is no defense against an infinite attack;

but never mind, let's find a hollow cove,
somewhere you can feel my warm pulse. Every
moment is a makeshift home. Temporary, travelling
time, which does not slip as steadily as glass would
have you believe, which instead sometimes heaves
and gives into gravity like autumn leaves. All at once,
you love me all at once, you love me in every form, your
shapeshifting daughter, who outgrows worlds before your eyes
like flowers that rush to offer their insides
up to the sun.

To the sun.

《水的边缘》

如果这不是真实的,
海滩上会有更多的沙子,
更少的卵石。
水推动一场艰难的
交易,
这缓慢而消耗精力的解体。
碎片堆积,
叠叠木的脊椎裂开了。
我知道,
您在最后的站立中摇摇欲坠。
对无尽的攻击疲于防御。

但没关系,让我们找一个海湾,
在那里,您能感觉到我脉搏的温暖。
每一个时刻
都是临时的家。
流动的时间,
并非我们所相信的稳如玻璃。

它更像一片秋叶,
会在重力下突然飘落。
一刻间,
您在每一刻全心全意地爱着我,
以各种方式
爱着不断长大的女儿。
在您眼前,超越了世界,
如同急切绽放的花朵
朝着太阳。

奔向太阳。

World-Ending

There is important work to do.
Pain, like fruit, must be born.
Dangling from my fingertips;
I am fertile, full of sorrow,
you will find my grief as clean and sweet
as the freshwater brook that tumbles over
rockfall. You will drink from it, the woven
finger goblet, silver fish streaming past your knuckles.
Amazement;

who knew life could be like this,
where every disaster edges closer
on the horizon like a sun-god, gripping
blood-orange fistfuls. It will come,
the end of the world. If I think I am ready

to be set aflame, then it does not know.
It cannot hear the fluting in my throat,
only the round circumference of my oak,
the way I promise to burn.

《世界末日》

有重要的工作要做。
痛苦，就像必然成熟的果实，
在我指尖摇曳。
我的悲伤已经成熟，
您会发现我的痛苦是甘甜而纯净的，
宛如清泉在陡峭岩石上流淌。
您可以用编织的高脚杯
品味其中，
任由银色的鱼儿掠过指缝。
惊愕，

谁承想生活会这样？
每一个灾难都从地平线上逼近，
如同太阳神一样，
紧扣着血橙色的拳头。
它将会降临，
世界末日。

如果我已准备好被点燃，
那它并不知道。
它听不到我喉间的低语，
只看到我橡树的周身，
我承诺要燃烧的方式。

Volcano

For years I could only spell my name.
Then comes this childish articulation,
a poetic language reduced to clumsy garble,
wholly learnt for loving you:

Mama bao bao deng yi deng bie zou.

《火山》

早些年, 我只会拼写自己的名字。
随之而来的是稚嫩的童音,
诗句被简化成含混的咿咿呀呀,
因为爱您, 我学会了说:

妈妈, 抱抱, 等一等, 别走。

Permafrost

Couldn't feel anything. Opened my eyes
to snow, the polar wind, no
music. The wild white wilderness
of disbelieving grief. How it strips
everything of meaning and forces
new ways to live. There is nothing green here.

When everyone has left me,
my love, when you leave
I will still be here, wading through routine.
I can't feel my hands or feet. Before I evolve
let me be human a little longer, before scarcity
ices over.

《冰封世界》

一切都失去了感觉，
我睁开眼睛，
看到的是冰雪、极地的寒风，没有音乐。
野性的白色荒原，
充满了难以言喻的悲痛。
一层层剥离
所有的意义和力量。
这是一种不同的生活，
没有一丝绿意。

当每个人都离我而去时，
我的爱，当您离去时，
我仍将在此，度过例行的日子。
我感受不到自己的手或脚。
在我进化之前，
在枯竭冰冻之先，
请多给我一点时间，
让我像人一样，活着。

Soft

There is nothing to ask for.
Grief is so clean, it rearranges
the parts of me I can't see
like surgery. The metal, cool against
the illuminated tissue. Quivering. I am
another object. It means nothing.

The world shifts around you,
the lines in its fabric pointing towards
where you rest. How you make even death
like love, cradling it so it won't hurt me.
How you plan to protect me from beyond it.

And I'll let you.

I do not struggle. I want to be
brave, a good woman, someone
that love can grow upwards from
even laying down. I am on the ground;
I don't fight. You tell me you will fight.
You promise not to give up, but you

deserve to rest, if not now, then then.
Do not give up and I will not give up either;
I am someone you can rely on. I love you so widely
I can let death be soft.

《柔和》

我不奢求什么,
悲伤如此纯净,
它重新塑造了
我无形的身躯。
像外科手术的金属刀,
切入那闪烁的血肉。
颤抖着,我成为
另一个存在,
却毫不介怀。

世界围绕着您转动,
编织的线条指向
您休憩的地方。
您居然想把死亡变成爱,
轻晃着它的摇篮,
不让其伤害我。
您计划如何守护我。

我由着您。

我想要成为一个
勇敢的女人,
即使身体已倒下,
爱依然升起。
我在地上; 我不抵抗。
您告诉我您会抗争到底。
虽然您需要休息,
现在, 或将来。

您不放弃, 我亦不会。
我是您可以信赖的人。
我太爱您了,
愿接纳死亡的柔和。

Buddhist Mantra

Like mother like daughter like
mother like daughter like mother
like daughter like mother like
daughter like mother like
mother like daughter.

《佛经》

如母如女如
母如女如母
如女如母如
女如母如
母如女。

Adolescence

Maybe you never thought
it would ever really come,
the white house and ocean
and second child. A husband
and son at either end of the
dinner table, us in the middle.
In Scotland, the world cracks open
for your pleasure, a sprawling halcyon
of farm animals, air you can breathe in deep.
Something dances out of your adolescence;
the whisper of a translated novel, where people
exchange mandarin on the other side of the globe. I cannot speak
for a life I did not live. I only know Glasgow,
where the children speak, accented,
teaching me the lesson of solitude. I suppose I never thought
it would ever really come, the day I was truly alone.

《青春期》

也许您从没想过
这一生真的会有
一座白房子、海,
和第二个孩子。
丈夫和儿子在餐桌两端,
您我坐在中间。
在苏格兰, 世界为您欣然敞开,
带来无尽的愉悦。
蔓延的宁静,
农场的动物,
还有清新的空气让我们深深地呼吸。
有什么在您的青春期舞动?
在翻译的小说中
人们悄悄地,
在地球的另一边交换着普通话。
我无法评论
我没有经历过的人生。
我只知道格拉斯哥,
和孩子们的口音。
学会了独处。
但从没想过,
这一天会真实降临,

当我彻底孤独。

Saturday Evening

I came home.
We cooked dumplings –
green beans, mushroom, and tofu
folded in powdered skin, boiled
from the outside in. The way I had
to fight you from the sink, one arm
on the frying pan, the other gloved,
laughing. Don't do the washing up,
relax, sit down. Relax. Let me

grow stronger, get better at
cleaning the kitchen, preparing yoghurt,
chopping vegetables. Thinking
that even if you live to ninety,
one day I will need to look after you.
I would want to know how to.

Yet even now –
it wasn't until I saw your face,
smelt the lotion on your cheeks
that the fear was pierced, like a
needle to a balloon. Even now
you understand the best.

《周六的傍晚》

我回家了。
我们煮饺子 –
绿豆芽、蘑菇和豆腐
包裹在扑粉的饺子皮里, 煮熟。
我与您争夺水槽,
一只手握着炒锅,
另一只戴着手套,
大笑着。
不需要您洗碗,
放松下来, 坐下。放松。
让我

变得更坚强,
更擅长
厨房的打理,
准备酸奶。
切蔬菜。
心想,
即使您活到九十岁,
总有一天我需要照顾您。
我会想知道如何做。

然而, 即使此刻,
当我看到您的脸庞,
闻到您脸颊上的芬芳,
恐惧像针扎进气球。
瞬间被刺穿。
即使此刻,
您仍然最懂我。

Bedtime

Low voices carry into the kitchen.
I had finished rinsing the sink,
so heard her,

I used to come home every night and cry.

Wanted to lie, but you see it
and know better than me.
Like you said on the plane home from China
no one can replace a mother. Like you say
everyone else will eventually be on their way
but I am still only little,
standing in the window of light behind the door
of your bedroom, lingering. You need to sleep
but I won't leave. April, go to bed. Cuddle your
toy animal. Pretend it is me.

《就寝时间》

低声细语传入厨房。
我已经洗完碗碟,
听到了她的声音。

我过去每晚回家都哭泣。

想掩盖, 但您看穿了
比我更明白。
就像您在从中国回家的飞机上所说
没有人能取代母亲。
就像您所说的,
其他人最终都会离开。
但我还只是个小孩子,
站在门后,
您卧室的窗外, 徘徊。
您需要休息
而我却不舍离去。
April, 去睡吧。
抱着你的玩具动物,
假装它是我。

Bay Window

And time
couldn't pass more slowly.
The difficulty
of momentum, the only creature
that resists gravity. If it had things its way
I would be in the ground. Already

I am grown. No one knows
how long this part goes
on for, when it all
runs out. Let me
light a candle
and bring it
to the temple
where God waits
in silken shadows.

I remember now;
a dream, where I begged
for your life on my knees. By the
bay window, in the blue light,
a bedroom I wasn't allowed in. I
begged. I would do it again. Prayer
keeps cutting into my body, wind whipping
the long grass in half. Give me even the smallest hope
that you will come back
and I will follow its trail like a field mouse,
hungry, senseless, unable to give it up.

《凸窗》

时间
走得不能再慢。
艰难的惯性，是唯一
抵抗重力的东西。
如果依了后者，
我早已倒地。

我已长大。
没人知道
这一切会持续多久，
何时终结。
让我
点燃一支蜡烛，
带上它
前往寺庙，
那是上帝在。
丝绸般的阴影中等待。

回忆一个梦，
梦中我跪乞
您的生命。
在凸窗旁，蓝光下，
那个不允许我进入的卧室。
我祈求着，
再一次祈求。
祈祷
不断地切入我的身体，
如长风割断草。
即使给我最微小的希望，
说您会回来。
我也会像田鼠一样，
追逐希望的踪迹，
饥饿，失去理智，
但无法放弃。

Photosynthesis

To the sun – I come –
I raise up – I release sepal, find
all my petals, I – lift, tilt, seek out –
look around, bend over myself – try
to find. This water is painfully needed,
each drop heavy enough to bruise. One day
I will lose. I will lose. I will return
into the ground and I will not come out. Not I.

But you,
you are in the sky. Glorious, life-giving
sound, and I think I hear –
vibrations like –
golden bells, the sound
of a loved one arriving,
coming into reach,
bearing another gift,
speaking to me without a mouth.
I don't need ears to listen. I have found
new, brilliant communication.

《光合作用》

向着太阳— 我来了
我升起来—释放萼片,
找到我所有的花瓣,
我向上, 倾斜, 寻找 —
环顾四周, 弯下腰
试着寻找。
我渴望水,
滴滴沉重,
足以致伤。
有一天
我将会输。
我将会输。
我会回归大地,
不再出现。
我无法前进。

但是您,
您在天空中。
辉煌的、赋予生命的声音,
我想我听到了—
震动如金钟。

声音
是心爱的人到来,
走近,
带着另一份礼物,
无需开口与我交谈。
无需耳朵我能倾听。
我找到了
一种崭新的、奇妙的沟通方式。

Mugdock

A familiar road.
In my dreams
I follow from Milngavie
to the castle. Round to where
the swans bring forth the smallest
cygnets. Barely able to stand on two feet.
Give me

a car park and I will find a way in.
I will never stop walking in the direction
you gave me. There is kindness in the leaves,
swallowing sun as if it is their last opportunity.
I could say love is eternal

but I will never live long enough to know.
These memories will die with me, and will
then grow amnesia, new space to remember
other green places. Until then, know

that there was nothing sweeter I would have
chosen for my few, blossoming moments –
nothing sweeter. No one dearer.

《玛格达克乡村公园》

一条熟悉的路,
在我的梦中。
我从米尔加出发,
走去公园的城堡。
那里的天鹅孵化出微小的幼崽,
它们几乎无法站立。
给我

一个停车场,
我会找到进入的路。
我永远不会停止,
朝着您所指示的方向前行。
树叶怀着善意, 咽下阳光,
仿佛这是它们最后的机会。
我敢说爱是永恒的

但我永远不会活那么久去验证。
这些记忆将与我一同逝去,
然后长出遗忘的苔藓,
为新的记忆空间腾出地方,
为其他绿洲。
在那之前, 我知道

没有什么比这份回忆更甜蜜。
是的, 在我为数不多的、
鲜花盛开的日子里,
没有什么比这更甜蜜,
没有人比您更亲密。

Regeneration

And we are back, again
at the beginning.

When your mother died
I promised you would always have me
at least. I keep
everything you gave me. I keep
it warm for another generation.
Daughter, I am already sorry.

The bed looks different from the right side.

This painful turnover of family. Quiet
in the living room so my father and I
don't hear each other's hearts breaking.
The water still runs after the dishes are done.
It will run all the way home to the ocean,
before ascending to a world where I can't
follow you.

Yet. The truth is I have no idea
when I'm coming home, or where
the water goes. Just know
that even though she is gone
I will be right beside you
until the very end.

《重生》

我们再次，
回到起点。

当您的母亲去世时
我承诺过，
至少您将永远拥有我。
我为下一代人保留温暖。
我的女儿，我对你已感到抱歉。

床还是床，但看起来不同了。

这痛苦的家庭更替。
在客厅里，我们默默无声
这样父亲和我就听不到彼此心碎的声音。
洗完的盘子，水仍然在流淌。
它将一直奔向大海，
然后升到一个
我无法跟随的世界。

事实上，我不知道，
我何时会回家？
或者水将流向何方？
我只知道，即使它已经离去，
我仍然会守护着您，
直到时间的尽头。

A Daughter's letter to her Mother:

What can I say that I have not already told you? I remember sitting on the sofa with you when I was a teenager. It was a normal grey Scottish evening and I told you that the love you have given me has been the greatest gift in my life. I think I embarrassed you a little, but I felt I had to say it at least once. Your love has saved me over and over. Your love has saved me from things that haven't even happened yet.

I was only nineteen when you were first diagnosed with lung cancer. I went home to my University flat, fought with my partner, and then sobbed over the bathroom sink for hours. I never told you about it. I think since then, I started to tell you less because I didn't want you to worry about me. When your cancer recurred after multiple surgeries and you were diagnosed for the second time, I was twenty-one. I sank to the floor of my flat in Dundee and said nothing for a long time. I used to cry before I slept and when I woke.

You told me you intended to live for me. For my father and for our family. You are a miraculous being. Never in my life, not even now, have I met anyone with such resilience, hope, strength, and love kernelled within their soul. How is it you have managed to live such a long, beautiful, peaceful life even with all the cards you have been dealt?

Because of you, I am the woman I am. I am able to love deeply, to care gently, to always persist. When I was a child, I thought if you ever died, I would die too. I feel a different truth now – that a mother is forever. Our love for each other will live forever. I am no longer afraid of the rest of my life, but welcome it, as you have welcomed yours.

I hope that this book has made you proud.

You always said that I reminded you of your mother, whom I am named after. I dedicate this book to her too, 肖亮华, for what she gave both of us. In another life, perhaps you are my daughter. All I know is that what has been given is always returned, reborn – and felt once again.

With all my heart, always,
April

女儿致母亲的信:

我还能说些什么, 除了已经告诉过您的?记得我还是少年时, 我们坐在沙发上。那是一个普通的苏格兰灰色傍晚, 我说, 您给我的爱是我一生中最伟大的礼物。我想我有点让您难为情, 但我觉得我至少应该告诉您一次。您的爱一次又一次救赎了我, 甚至把我从尚未发生的事件中救赎。

当您第一次被诊断出肺癌时, 我只有十九岁。我回到我大学的公寓, 和我的伴侣争吵, 然后在浴室的水槽边哭了几个小时。我从未告诉过您。我想从那时起, 我就开始少说一些事情 —— 不想让您担心我。当您肺癌术后复发时, 我二十一岁, 跌坐在邓迪的学生公寓地上, 久久地失语。那时我常在入睡和醒来时哭泣。

您告诉我, 为了我, 为了父亲和我们全家, 您要活下去。您是一个奇迹般的存在。在我的一生中, 即使是现在, 我也从未遇到过任何一个人像您一样, 灵魂核含了这么多坚韧、希望、力量和爱。您是如何设法过着如此漫长、美丽、平和的生活, 即使面临着所有的艰难?

因为您, 我成为了现在的我。我能够深爱、温柔地关怀、始终坚韧。当我还是个孩子时, 我以为如果您去世了, 我也会死。现在我感受到了不同的真相——一位母亲是永恒的。我们对彼此的爱将永存。我不再害怕余生, 而是像您一样欢迎它。

我希望这本书让您感到骄傲。

您总是说我让您想起了您的母亲, 我就是以她的名字命名的。我也将这本书献给她, 肖亮华, 为了她给我们两个人带来的一切。在另一种生活中, 也许您是我的女儿。我所知道的是, 所给予的总会被回报, 重生——并重新体验一切。

您全心全意, 永远的,
April

ACKNOWLEDGEMENTS

I want to thank Stuart Bartholomew and the team at VERVE Poetry Press for being so considerate with this body of work. I'm very appreciative of the effort it has taken to bring it into the world.

I need to thank my father, who has been just as important a role model for me as my mother. Thank you for always being so grounded, kind, and clever, particularly during the last few years, which have brought unprecedented challenges. I could not have gotten through some of these challenges without your support and strength.

I want to thank my brother, for being there when I needed him most.

I also need to thank my community and particularly my best friends, Kim, Chessy, and Rae. You are my chosen family and I am eternally grateful to have three such generous people by my side. You inspire me, make me laugh, encourage me to grow in all the ways. Whatever we go through, we go through it together!

Thank you Lily, my beautiful girlfriend, who has taken each hardship in stride and never faltered in loving me. Thank you for being so kind to my mum and to my family. You give me so much hope for the future.

Of course, thank you Mum, for everything. You will always be with me. Rest in peace.

ABOUT VERVE POETRY PRESS

Verve Poetry Press is an award-winning press which focussed initially on meeting a local need in Birmingham - a need for the vibrant poetry scene here in Brum to find a way to present itself to the poetry world via publication. Co-founded by Stuart Bartholomew and Amerah Saleh, it now publishes poets from all corners of the UK and beyond - poets that speak to the city's varied and energetic qualities and will contribute to its many poetic stories.

Added to this is a colourful pamphlet series, many featuring poets who have performed at our sister festival - and a poetry show series which captures the magic of longer poetry performance pieces by festival alumni such as Polarbear, Suhaiymah Manzour-Khan and Imogen Stirling.

The press has been voted Most Innovative Publisher at the Saboteur Awards, and has won the Publisher's Award for Poetry Pamphlets at the Michael Marks Awards.

Like the festival, we strive to think about poetry in inclusive ways and embrace the multiplicity of approaches towards this glorious art.

https://vervepoetrypress.com
@VervePoetryPres
mail@vervepoetrypress.com